I0017767

Conquer Python

A Comprehensive Guide to Mastering the Language

Benjamin Evans

Copyright © 2024 Benjamin Evans

All rights reserved.

DEDICATION

To the relentless seekers of knowledge, the curious minds tirelessly decoding the mysteries of algorithms and code. This book is dedicated to you, the coders who embrace the challenges of neural networks with fervor and determination. May these pages serve as stepping stones on your journey, empowering you to unravel the complexities of this dynamic field and craft solutions that shape the future. Your passion fuels the innovation that drives our world forward, and for that, I extend my deepest gratitude and admiration.

CONTENTS

ACKNOWLEDGMENTS

I would like to extend my sincere gratitude to all those who have contributed to the realization of this book. First and foremost, I am indebted to my family for their unwavering support and encouragement throughout this endeavor. Their love and understanding have been my anchor in the stormy seas of writing.

I am deeply thankful to the experts whose guidance and insights have illuminated my path and enriched the content of this book. Their mentorship has been invaluable in shaping my understanding and refining my ideas.

I also extend my appreciation to those whose constructive feedback and insightful suggestions have helped polish this work to its finest form.

Furthermore, I am grateful to the countless individuals whose research, publications, and contributions have paved the way for the insights shared in these pages.

Last but not least, I express my heartfelt appreciation to the readers who embark on this journey with me. Your curiosity and engagement breathe life into these words, and it is for you that this book exists.

Thank you all for being part of this remarkable journey.

CHAPTER 1

INTRODUCTION TO PYTHON

Welcome to the exciting world of Python programming! This chapter will lay the foundation for your Python journey, introducing you to what Python is, why it's an excellent choice for beginners and professionals alike, how to set up your development environment, and finally, the fundamentals of Python syntax, including variables, data types, and operators.

1.1 What is Python?

Python is a high-level, general-purpose programming language known for its readability, simplicity, and versatility. Unlike some programming languages with complex syntax, Python reads almost like natural language, making it easier to learn and understand. This focus on readability combined with its powerful features makes Python a popular choice for a wide range of applications, including:

- **Web Development:** Python frameworks like Django and Flask power some of the most popular websites today.
- **Data Science and Machine Learning:** Libraries like NumPy, Pandas, and Scikit-learn make Python a leader in data analysis and building intelligent systems.
- **Automation:** Scripting repetitive tasks with Python can save you significant time and effort.
- **Game Development:** Python frameworks like Pygame allow you to create engaging games.
- **Scientific Computing:** Python is widely used for scientific calculations and simulations.
- **General-Purpose Programming:** From desktop applications to system administration, Python can be used for a vast array of tasks.

1.2 Why Learn Python?

There are numerous reasons why Python is an excellent

choice for anyone considering learning to code. Here are some key benefits:

- **Beginner-friendly:** Python's clear syntax and focus on readability make it easier to learn compared to languages with complex syntax.
- **Versatility:** Python's wide range of applications makes it a valuable skill for various career paths.
- **Large and Active Community:** Python boasts a vast and supportive community of developers, offering extensive resources and help online.
- **Open-Source and Free:** Python is an open-source language, meaning it's free to use and modify, making it accessible to everyone.
- **Abundant Libraries and Frameworks:** Python has a rich ecosystem of libraries and frameworks, providing ready-made tools for various tasks.

Whether you're a complete beginner, an experienced programmer looking to expand your skills, or someone seeking a powerful tool for specific tasks, Python is an excellent language to learn.

1.3 Setting Up Your Development Environment

To start writing Python code, you'll need a development environment. Here are the essential components:

- **Text Editor or IDE:** A text editor like Sublime Text or an Integrated Development Environment (IDE) like PyCharm offers features like syntax highlighting, code completion, and debugging tools to make writing code more efficient.

- **Python Interpreter:** This is the program that executes your Python code. You can download the latest Python version from the official website (https://www.python.org/downloads/). When installed, the interpreter comes bundled with a simple text-based IDE called IDLE.

Here's how to check if Python is installed on your system (using a command prompt/terminal):

Windows:

py --version

Mac/Linux:

python3 --version

If Python is installed, the command will display the installed version. If not, download and install it from the official website.

Using an IDE like PyCharm:

1. Download and install PyCharm from https://www.jetbrains.com/pycharm/.
2. Open PyCharm and create a new Python project.
3. Start writing your Python code in the editor. PyCharm provides various features to assist you.

Using IDLE (bundled with Python):

1. Open IDLE (usually found in your start menu/applications folder).
2. The main window provides a text editor for writing your code.
3. Execute your code by pressing F5 or selecting "Run" -> "Run Module".

1.4 Basic Python Syntax: Variables, Data Types, Operators

Now that you have your development environment set up, let's explore the fundamental building blocks of Python programs: variables, data types, and operators.

1.4.1 Variables:

Variables are named containers that store data in your program. You can think of them like labeled boxes where you can hold information. To create a variable, you simply assign a name to a value using the assignment operator (=). Here's an example:

```
name = "Alice"
age = 30
```

In this example, we create two variables: name and age. We assign the string "Alice" to the name variable and the integer 30 to the age variable.

Variable Naming Rules:

- Variable names can consist of letters (uppercase and lowercase), numbers, and underscores (_).
- The first character must be a letter or an underscore.

CHAPTER 2

CONTROL FLOW

we delve into the world of control flow, which determines the order in which your program executes instructions. Control flow allows you to make decisions based on conditions and repeat specific code blocks as needed.

2.1 Conditional Statements: if/else, elif

Conditional statements, also known as branching statements, allow your program to execute different code blocks based on whether a condition is true or false. Python offers two primary conditional statements: if and else.

- **if statement:** This statement checks a condition. If the condition is true, the code block is indented after the if statement is executed.

```
age = 15
```

```
if age >= 18:
  print("You are eligible to vote.")
else:
  print("You are not eligible to vote.")
```

In this example, the program checks if the age variable is greater than or equal to 18. If it is, the message "You are eligible to vote" is printed. Otherwise, the message "You are not eligible to vote" is printed.

- **else statement:** The else statement provides an alternative block of code to execute if the condition in the if statement is false.

elif statement:

Sometimes, you may need to check multiple conditions. Python offers the elif statement (else if) for chaining multiple conditional checks within a single if statement block.

```
grade = 85
```

```python
if grade >= 90:
  print("Excellent!")
elif grade >= 80:
  print("Very Good!")
else:
  print("Good luck next time!")
```

Here, the program checks the value of the grade variable. If it's 90 or above, "Excellent!" is printed. If it's between 80 and 89 (after the first condition fails), "Very Good!" is printed. Otherwise, the else block executes, printing "Good luck next time!"

2.2 Loops: for, while

Loops allow you to execute a block of code repeatedly until a certain condition is met. Python provides two main types of loops: for loops and while loops.

- **for loop:** This loop iterates over a sequence of items (like a list or string) and executes a block of code for each item.

```
fruits = ["apple", "banana", "cherry"]

for fruit in fruits:
    print(fruit)
```

This code iterates through the fruits list, printing each fruit name on a new line. The for loop variable (fruit in this case) takes on the value of each item in the sequence during each iteration.

- **while loop:** This loop continues to execute a block of code as long as a certain condition remains true.

```
count = 0

while count < 5:
    print(count)
    count += 1
```

This code uses a while loop to print numbers from 0 to 4. The count variable is incremented by 1 within the loop, and the loop continues as long as count is less than 5. Once count reaches 5, the condition becomes false, and the loop terminates.

2.3 Functions: Defining and Calling Functions

Functions are reusable blocks of code that perform specific tasks. They promote code modularity and make your programs more organized and easier to maintain.

- **Defining a function:** You define a function using the def keyword, followed by the function name and parentheses. The indented block of code below the function definition defines the code to be executed when the function is called.

```
def greet(name):
    """This function greets a person by name."""
    print("Hello,", name + "!")


greet("Alice")
```

In this example, we define a function called greet that takes a name as input. The function body prints a greeting message using the provided name. We then call the greet function with the argument "Alice," which executes the function and prints "Hello, Alice!"

- **Calling a function:** You call a function using its name followed by parentheses. Any arguments required by the function are passed within the parentheses.

```
def calculate_area(length, width):
    """This function calculates the area of a rectangle."""
    area = length * width
    return area


result = calculate_area(5, 10)
print(result)  # Output: 50
```

- **Global Scope:** Variables defined outside any function are considered global and are accessible from anywhere within the program, including inside functions.

```python
global_var = "This is a global variable"

def access_global_var():
    print(global_var)   # Accessing global variable inside a
function

access_global_var() # Output: This is a global variable

# Modifying a global variable inside a function
def modify_global_var():
    global global_var  # Declare global keyword to modify
    global_var = "Global variable modified!"

modify_global_var()
print(global_var) # Output: Global variable modified!
```

Key Points about Scope and Lifetime:

- Local variables are created when a function is called and destroyed when the function finishes execution.

- Global variables exist throughout the entire program's lifetime. Use global variables with caution as they can lead to unintended side effects if modified within functions.

- It's generally recommended to prioritize local variables and function arguments to keep your code modular and easier to understand.

Additional Concepts:

- **Variable Lifetime:** The lifetime of a variable refers to the period during which it exists in memory. Local variables have a lifetime limited to the function's execution, while global variables exist throughout the program's lifetime.

- **Name Shadowing:** When a local variable has the same name as a global variable, the local variable takes precedence within the function's scope. This can be confusing, so it's best to avoid using the same names for local and global variables.

By understanding scope and lifetime, you can write cleaner, more maintainable Python code.

CHAPTER 3

DATA STRUCTURES

These structures provide efficient ways to manage various types of data and perform operations on them.

3.1 Lists: Creating, Accessing, Modifying Lists

Lists are mutable ordered sequences of elements. They are versatile and widely used to store collections of items. Here's how to work with lists:

- **Creating Lists:** You can create a list using square brackets [] and enclosing the elements separated by commas.

```
fruits = ["apple", "banana", "cherry"]
numbers = [1, 2, 3, 4, 5]
```

- **Accessing Elements:** Elements in a list are indexed

starting from 0. You can access individual elements using their index within square brackets.

first_fruit = fruits[0] # first_fruit will be "apple"
second_number = numbers[1] # second_number will be 2

- **Negative Indexing:** You can access elements from the end of the list using negative indexing, starting from -1 for the last element.

last_fruit = fruits[-1] # last_fruit will be "cherry"

- **Slicing:** You can extract a portion of a list using slicing. Slicing uses a colon : to specify the start and end index (end index is exclusive).

sublist = fruits[1:3] # sublist will be ["banana", "cherry"] (elements at index 1 and 2)

- **Modifying Lists:** Lists are mutable, meaning you

can change their contents after creation. You can modify elements by assigning a new value to their index.

```
fruits[0] = "mango"  # Modifying the first element
fruits.append("orange")  # Adding an element to the end
using append()
```

- **Common List Methods:** Python provides various methods for manipulating lists. Here are a few examples:

  - len(list): Returns the length (number of elements) of the list.
  - list.insert(index, element): Inserts an element at a specific index.
  - list.remove(element): Removes the first occurrence of an element.
  - list.pop(index): Removes and returns the element at a specific index (or the last element by default).

Lists are a powerful and flexible data structure for storing and managing ordered collections of items. They can hold elements of different data types, making them highly adaptable for various tasks.

3.2 Tuples: Immutable Ordered Sequences

Tuples are similar to lists but are immutable, meaning their elements cannot be changed after creation. They are defined using parentheses (). Here's what you need to know about tuples:

- **Creating Tuples:**

coordinates = (3, 5) # A tuple containing x and y coordinates
empty_tuple = () # An empty tuple

- **Accessing Elements:** Tuples use the same indexing scheme as lists for accessing elements.

x_coordinate = coordinates[0] # x_coordinate will be 3

- **Immutability:** Unlike lists, you cannot modify elements within a tuple after its creation.

This will cause an error: coordinates[0] = 10

Tuples are often used for data that should remain constant throughout the program, such as coordinates or configuration settings. They provide a way to group related elements while ensuring data integrity.

3.3 Dictionaries: Key-Value Pairs for Data Storage

Dictionaries, also known as associative arrays, store data using key-value pairs. Unlike lists and tuples, which use numerical indexes, dictionaries access elements using unique keys. This makes them ideal for storing and retrieving data based on descriptive names or identifiers.

- **Creating Dictionaries:** Dictionaries are enclosed in curly braces {} and use a colon : to separate keys and values. Keys can be strings or numbers, while values can be any data type.

```
person = {
  "name": "Alice",
  "age": 30,
  "city": "New York"
}

# Accessing elements using keys
name = person["name"]  # name will be "Alice"
```

- **Adding and Modifying Elements:** You can add new key-value pairs or modify existing values by assigning them within the dictionary structure.

```
person["occupation"] = "Software Engineer"  # Adding a new key-value pair
person["age"]
```

3.4 Sets: Unique Elements and Set Operations

Sets are unordered collections of unique elements. They are useful for storing collections where order doesn't matter and you only want to keep distinct values. Sets are created using curly braces {} but unlike dictionaries, they don't have key-value pairs.

- **Creating Sets:**

```
unique_fruits = {"apple", "banana", "cherry", "cherry"}
# Duplicates are removed

numbers_set = set([1, 2, 2, 3, 4])  # Set creation from a list (duplicates removed)
```

- **Accessing Elements:** Since sets are unordered, you cannot access elements by index. However, you can check for membership using the in operator.

```
if "apple" in unique_fruits:
```

```
print("Apple is present in the set.")
```

- **Adding and Removing Elements:** You can add elements (must be unique) using the add() method and remove elements using the remove() or discard() methods.

```
unique_fruits.add("mango")  # Adding a new element

unique_fruits.remove("banana")     #  Removing  an
element (raises an error if not found)
unique_fruits.discard("grape")   # Attempts to remove
"grape" (doesn't raise an error if not found)
```

- **Set Operations:** Sets offer various operations for working with collections of elements. Here are some common ones:

  - union (|): Returns a new set containing all unique elements from both sets.

- o intersection (&): Returns a new set containing elements common to both sets.
- o difference (-): Returns a new set containing elements in the first set but not in the second.
- o isdisjoint (disjoint): Returns True if the sets have no common elements.

set1 = {1, 2, 3}
set2 = {3, 4, 5}

combined_set = set1 | set2 # combined_set will be {1, 2, 3, 4, 5}
    shared_elements = set1 & set2 # shared_elements will be {3}
    difference_set = set1 - set2 # difference_set will be {1, 2}
    are_disjoint = set1.isdisjoint(set2) # False (they share element 3)

Sets are efficient for tasks like removing duplicates from a list, checking for membership, and performing set-based operations.

Data structures are fundamental tools for organizing and managing data in Python programs. Lists provide ordered, mutable collections, while tuples offer immutable ordered sequences. Dictionaries excel at storing and retrieving data by key-value pairs. Finally, sets are ideal for handling unique elements and performing set operations. Choosing the right data structure depends on the specific needs of your program and the type of data you're working with.

Additional Considerations:

- Nested data structures: You can create data structures within other data structures. For example, a list can contain dictionaries, and a dictionary can contain lists.
- Choosing the right data structure: The choice of data structure depends on your program's needs. Consider factors like mutability, ordering, uniqueness of elements, and access methods.

- Performance considerations: Different data structures have varying performance characteristics for different operations. Understanding these aspects can help you optimize your code.

By mastering data structures, you'll be well-equipped to write efficient and well-organized Python programs.

CHAPTER 4

OBJECT-ORIENTED PROGRAMMING (OOP)

Object-oriented programming (OOP) is a programming paradigm that focuses on objects rather than procedures. Objects encapsulate data (attributes) and related operations (methods) that act upon that data. This approach promotes code modularity, reusability, and maintainability.

4.1 Classes and Objects: Defining Classes and Creating Objects

- **Classes:** A class acts as a blueprint for creating objects. It defines the attributes (variables) and methods (functions) that objects of that class will possess. You can think of a class as a template for creating specific instances.

```python
class Car:
    """A simple Car class."""
```

```
    def __init__(self, make, model, year):  # Constructor
method
        self.make = make
        self.model = model
        self.year = year

    def accelerate(self):
        print("The car is accelerating!")

    # Creating objects (instances) of the Car class
    my_car = Car("Ford", "Mustang", 2023)
    another_car = Car("Toyota", "Camry", 2022)

    print(my_car.make)  # Output: Ford
    my_car.accelerate()  # Output: The car is accelerating!
```

In this example, the Car class defines attributes like make, model, and year, along with a method called accelerate. We then create two objects, my_car and another_car, instances of the Car class. These objects have access to the defined attributes and methods.

- **Constructor Method (init):** The __init__ method (also known as the constructor) is a special method that is automatically called when you create an object of a class. It's used to initialize the object's attributes with starting values.

4.2 Inheritance: Creating Subclasses and Reusing Code

Inheritance allows you to create new classes (subclasses) that inherit attributes and methods from existing classes (parent classes). This promotes code reuse and simplifies the creation of related objects.

```python
class ElectricCar(Car):
    """A subclass of Car, specifically for electric vehicles."""

    def __init__(self, make, model, year, battery_size):
        super().__init__(make, model, year)  # Inheriting
```

attributes from Car

```
    self.battery_size = battery_size

  def charge(self):
    print("The electric car is charging.")

  electric_car = ElectricCar("Tesla", "Model S", 2024, 85)
  electric_car.accelerate()  # Inherited from Car
  electric_car.charge()  # Specific method of ElectricCar
```

Here, the ElectricCar class inherits from the Car class. It reuses the existing attributes (make, model, and year) and adds its own attribute (battery_size). Additionally, it defines a specific method called charge. The super().__init__(make, model, year) line ensures that the parent class's constructor is called first to initialize its attributes.

4.3 Encapsulation: Protecting Data and Methods

Encapsulation is the concept of bundling data (attributes)

and methods together within a class, and controlling access to them. This allows you to protect sensitive data from unauthorized modification. Public, private, and protected access modifiers are used to define access levels:

- **Public:** Attributes and methods declared with no access modifier are considered public and can be accessed from anywhere in your program.
- **Private:** Attributes and methods prefixed with double underscores (＿＿) are considered private and are generally only accessible within the class itself (and potentially its subclasses).
- **Protected:** Attributes and methods prefixed with a single underscore (＿) are considered protected and can be accessed within the class and its subclasses, but not directly from outside the class hierarchy.

By default, Python uses public attributes and methods. However, you can control access to sensitive data using private or protected modifiers.

4.4 Polymorphism: Method Overriding and Duck

Typing

Polymorphism allows objects of different classes to respond to the same method call in different ways. This flexibility enhances code reusability and promotes dynamic behavior. Here are two key concepts:

- **Method Overriding:** When a subclass inherits a method from a parent class, it can define its own implementation of that method. This allows for specialized behavior for specific object types.

```python
class SportsCar(Car):
    """A subclass of Car with a custom accelerate method."""

    def accelerate(self):
      print("The sports car is accelerating rapidly!")

  # Calling accelerate on different objects
  my_car.accelerate()  # Output: The car is accelerating!
(inherited from Car)
```

```
sports_car = SportsCar("Ferrari", "F8 Tributo", 2023)
sports_car.accelerate()   # Output: The sports car is
accelerating rapidly! (overridden method)
```

In this example, the SportsCar class inherits the accelerate method from the Car class. However, it overrides the inherited behavior by defining its own accelerate method that prints a different message. This demonstrates how polymorphism allows for specialized behavior based on the object's type.

- **Duck Typing:** Duck typing is a concept in Python that focuses on whether an object has the required methods rather than its specific class. If an object has a method with the right name and arguments, it can be used in a certain context, regardless of its class hierarchy.

```
def make_sound(animal):
    """A function that expects an object with a
make_sound method."""
```

```
animal.make_sound()

# Create objects of different classes with a make_sound
method
dog = Dog()
cat = Cat()

make_sound(dog)  # Output: Woof! (from Dog class)
make_sound(cat)  # Output: Meow! (from Cat class)
```

Here, the make_sound function doesn't care what class the animal argument belongs to. As long as the object has a make_sound method, the function can call it. This approach promotes loose coupling between objects and makes code more flexible.

Object-oriented programming (OOP) provides a powerful way to structure your code using classes and objects. Inheritance allows for code reuse and creating specialized subclasses. Encapsulation helps protect data integrity, and polymorphism enables flexible method calls. By mastering these concepts, you can write well-organized, maintainable, and reusable Python programs.

CHAPTER 5

FILE HANDLING

Files are essential for storing and retrieving data persistently on your computer. Python provides mechanisms for working with various file formats to read, write, and manipulate data within your programs.

5.1 Reading and Writing Text Files

Text files are the simplest and most common file format. They store human-readable characters, often encoded in formats like UTF-8. Here's how to handle text files in Python:

- **Opening Files:** The open() function is used to open a file. It takes two main arguments:

    - filename (str): The path to the file you want to open.

    - mode (str): The mode in which you want to

open the file. Common modes include:

- 'r': Open for reading (default). Raises an error if the file doesn't exist.
- 'w': Open for writing. Creates a new file or overwrites an existing one.
- 'a': Open for appending. Adds content to the end of an existing file or creates a new file if it doesn't exist.
- 'r+': Open for both reading and writing. You can modify the file content.

```python
# Read a text file
with open("data.txt", "r") as file:
    contents = file.read()  # Reads the entire file content as a string
    print(contents)


# Write to a text file (overwrites existing content)
with open("data.txt", "w") as file:
    file.write("This is some new text data.")
```

- **Reading from Files:** Once a file is opened in read mode ('r'), you can use methods to access its content:

  - read(): Reads the entire file content as a string.
  - readline(): Reads a single line from the file as a string (including the newline character).
  - readlines(): Reads all lines from the file and stores them in a list of strings (without newline characters).

-

- **Writing to Files:** When a file is opened in write mode ('w') or append mode ('a'), you can use the write() method to add content:

  - write(str): Writes the given string content to the file.

-

Important: Always use the with statement when working with files. It ensures proper file closing even if exceptions occur.

5.2 Working with CSV and JSON Files

- **CSV (Comma-Separated Values) Files:** CSV files store tabular data where each row represents a record and columns are separated by commas. The csv module provides tools for reading and writing CSV data.

```python
import csv

# Read data from a CSV file
with open("data.csv", "r") as csvfile:
    reader = csv.reader(csvfile)
    for row in reader:
        print(row)  # Each row is a list containing cell values

# Write data to a CSV file
with open("data.csv", "w", newline="") as csvfile:
    writer = csv.writer(csvfile)
    writer.writerow(["Name", "Age", "City"])
    writer.writerow(["Alice", 30, "New York"])
```

- **JSON (JavaScript Object Notation) Files:** JSON files store data in a lightweight, human-readable format using key-value pairs. The json module helps you work with JSON data.

```python
import json

# Read data from a JSON file
with open("data.json", "r") as jsonfile:
    data = json.load(jsonfile) # Loads the JSON data into a
Python dictionary


# Write data to a JSON file
data = {"name": "Bob", "age": 25, "city": "London"}
with open("data.json", "w") as jsonfile:
    json.dump(data, jsonfile) # Dumps the Python
dictionary into a JSON file
```

These modules offer convenient ways to handle structured data formats like CSV and JSON, making data exchange and processing easier.

- **Try-Except Block:** The try-except block is used to enclose code that might raise exceptions. You can define specific exception handlers to catch and manage errors.

```
try:
  with open("missing_file.txt", "r") as file:
    contents = file.read()
except FileNotFoundError:
  print("Error: File 'missing_file.txt' not found.")
else:
  # Code to execute if no exceptions occur (optional)
finally:
  # Code to always execute, regardless of exceptions
(optional)
  # Useful for closing files or releasing resources
```

In this example, the try block attempts to open the file. If a FileNotFoundError occurs, the except block handles the error by printing a specific message. The else block (optional) executes code only if no exceptions occur. Finally, the finally block (optional) ensures that the file is closed, even if exceptions are raised.

- **Common File-Related Exceptions:**

    o FileNotFoundError: Raised when a file is not found.

    o PermissionError: Raised when you lack permission to access a file.

    o IOError: A general base class for input/output errors.

-

By using exception handling, you can make your code more robust and user-friendly, providing informative error messages when unexpected situations arise.

5.4 File System Navigation and Manipulation

The os module provides functionalities for interacting with the operating system's file system. Here are some common operations:

- **Getting File Path:**

```
import os

current_path = os.getcwd()   # Get the current working
directory
file_path = os.path.join(current_path, "data.txt")   # Join
path components
```

- **Checking File Existence:**

```
if os.path.exists("data.txt"):
  print("File 'data.txt' exists.")
else:
  print("File 'data.txt' does not exist.")
```

- **Creating Directories:**

```
os.makedirs("new_directory/subdirectory")    # Creates
nested directories if they don't exist
```

- **Renaming and Deleting Files:**

```
os.rename("old_file.txt", "new_file.txt")    # Rename a
file
os.remove("unwanted_file.txt") # Delete a file
```

Important: Use these functionalities with caution, as modifying the file system can have unintended consequences.

File handling in Python allows you to interact with various file formats for reading, writing, and manipulating data. By understanding how to work with text files, CSV, JSON, and using exception handling for error management, you can create versatile programs that interact with data stored on your computer's file system. The os module provides additional tools for navigating and manipulating the file system itself. Remember to exercise caution when modifying the file system to avoid unintended consequences.

CHAPTER 6

Modules and Packages

In Python, modules and packages are fundamental building blocks for code organization and reusability. They allow you to structure your code into logical units and share functionality across different parts of your program or even with other projects.

6.1 Importing Modules and Packages

- **Modules:** A module is a Python file (.py) containing functions, classes, variables, and other code statements. You can import modules into your program to use the defined functionalities.

```
import math

# Use functions from the math module
result = math.sqrt(16)  # result will be 4.0
```

```
print(result)
```

- **Importing Specific Functions/Classes:** You can import specific functions or classes from a module using the from ... import syntax.

```
from math import pi

# Use the pi constant from the math module
area = pi * radius**2
print(area)
```

- **Packages:** A package is a directory that contains multiple modules and potentially subdirectories (sub-packages). It provides a hierarchical structure for organizing related code.

```
import statistics  # Assuming statistics is a package in your project
```

```python
# Use a function from the statistics module
data = [2, 5, 7, 1, 8]
average = statistics.mean(data)
print(average)
```

Important: When using modules and packages from external sources, ensure they are installed in your Python environment.

6.2 Creating Your Own Modules and Packages

- **Creating Modules:** Save your code in a Python file (e.g., my_functions.py). This file becomes a module you can import into other programs.

```python
# my_functions.py
def greet(name):
  """Prints a greeting message."""
  print(f"Hello, {name}!")
```

```
def calculate_area(length, width):
    """Calculates the area of a rectangle."""
    return length * width
```

- **Importing Your Module:** In another Python file, you can import your module using import or from ... import.

```
# main_program.py
import my_functions

my_functions.greet("Alice")
area = my_functions.calculate_area(5, 3)
print(f"Area: {area}")
```

- **Packages:** Create a directory structure to organize your code. Within the directory (package name), you can have your main module (usually named __init__.py) and other sub-modules.

```
my_package/
```

__init__.py   # Optional initialization code for the package

calculations.py   # Module containing calculation functions

data_structures.py # Module containing data structure definitions

When using packages, ensure the package directory is located on your Python path or within the project structure for proper import.

6.3 Working with the Standard Library

Python comes with a rich standard library containing modules for various functionalities. You can explore the documentation (https://docs.python.org/) to find modules for tasks like:

- Mathematical operations (math)
- String manipulation (str)
- File handling (open, csv, json)

- Working with the operating system (os)
- Network programming (socket)
- Web scraping (requests)
- And many more!

The standard library provides a vast collection of pre-built functionality that you can leverage in your programs.

6.4 Using Third-Party Packages: Installation and Management

The Python Package Index (PyPI) (https://pypi.org/) is a repository containing thousands of third-party packages developed by the community. You can install these packages using the pip package manager, which is usually included with Python installations.

- **Installing Packages:** Open your terminal or command prompt and run:

pip install package_name

- **Importing Installed Packages:** Once installed, you

can import them into your program like any other module.

```
import numpy   # Assuming numpy is a third-party package

# Use functions from the numpy package
array = numpy.array([1, 2, 3])
print(array)
```

- **Package Management Tools:** Virtual environments and tools like pipenv or conda help manage package dependencies and isolate environments for different projects. Consider using these tools for better project organization and dependency management.

Modules and packages are essential for code organization, reusability, and sharing functionality. Leverage the standard library and explore third-party packages on PyPI to enhance your Python development capabilities. Remember to manage dependencies effectively using virtual environments or package management tools. By understanding these concepts, you can structure your code effectively and write maintainable Python programs.

CHAPTER 7

WEB DEVELOPMENT WITH PYTHON

Python excels in web development thanks to powerful frameworks like Flask and Django. These frameworks provide a foundation for building dynamic web applications with features like routing, templating, user interaction, and database access.

7.1 Introduction to Flask (or Django): A Web Framework

- **Web Frameworks:** Web frameworks offer a structured approach to building web applications. They handle low-level details like request processing, routing, and templating, allowing you to focus on the application logic and user experience.

We'll focus on Flask in this chapter, but concepts are similar for other frameworks like Django.

- **Flask:** Flask is a lightweight and flexible web framework. It provides essential tools for building web applications while allowing for customization and integration with other libraries.

Here's a brief comparison of Flask and Django:

Feature	Flask	Django
Complexity	Less complex, more flexibility	More complex, opinionated structure
Use Cases	Simple APIs, smaller projects	Complex web applications, rapid development
Learning Curve	Easier to learn for beginners	Steeper learning curve

Choosing a framework depends on your project's needs

and your familiarity with web development concepts.

7.2 Building Basic Web Applications with Routes and Templates

- **Routes:** Routes map URLs to specific functions in your application that handle incoming requests.

from flask import Flask, render_template

app = Flask(__name__)

@app.route("/") # Decorator defines the route for the root URL
def home():
    return render_template("index.html") # Render the home page template

if __name__ == "__main__":
    app.run(debug=True) # Run the application in debug mode

In this example, the @app.route("/") decorator defines a route for the root URL (/). When a user visits the homepage, the home function is called, and it renders the index.html template.

- **Templates:** Templates are HTML files with placeholders for dynamic content. Flask allows you to define these placeholders and populate them with data from your Python code.

HTML

```html
<!DOCTYPE html>
<html>
<head>
 <title>My Website</title>
</head>
<body>
 <h1>Welcome to {{ title }}!</h1>
</body>
</html>
```

Here, the {{ title }} placeholder will be replaced with the

value returned by the home function.

Flask provides powerful templating features to create dynamic and interactive web pages.

7.3 Handling User Input and Form Processing

- **Forms:** Web forms allow users to interact with your application by submitting data. Flask helps you process form submissions and access user input.

```
from flask import Flask, render_template, request

app = Flask(__name__)

@app.route("/", methods=["GET", "POST"])  # Handle
both GET and POST requests
    def home():
        if request.method == "POST":
            name = request.form["name"]  # Access form data by
name attribute
```

```
    return f"Hello, {name}!"
  else:
    return render_template("index.html")


if __name__ == "__main__":
  app.run(debug=True)
```

This example demonstrates handling both GET (initial page load) and POST (form submission) requests. The request.form["name"] retrieves the value submitted through the form's name field.

- **Validation and Sanitization:** It's crucial to validate user input to ensure data integrity and prevent security vulnerabilities. Flask provides tools and libraries for data validation and sanitization.

7.4 Working with Databases: Connecting and Interacting

- **Databases:** Web applications often need to store and

retrieve persistent data. Databases provide a structured way to manage this data.

Here's a simplified explanation of connecting and interacting with databases using Flask and an Object Relational Mapper (ORM):

1. **Choose a Database:** Popular choices include MySQL, PostgreSQL, and SQLite.
2. **Install an ORM:** An ORM simplifies database interaction by mapping database tables to Python objects. SQLAlchemy is a common ORM for Flask.
3. **Configure Database Connection:** Set up connection details (host, username, password) in your Flask application.
4. **Define Models:** Use SQLAlchemy to define models representing your database tables (e.g., User, Product).
5. **Interact with Data:** Use methods provided by the ORM to create, read, update, and delete data in the database.

Database interaction in Flask involves additional libraries and configuration.

CHAPTER 8

DATA SCIENCE WITH PYTHON

Python has become a dominant language in the field of data science due to its powerful libraries and ease of use. This chapter introduces essential tools and concepts for data analysis and machine learning.

8.1 Introduction to NumPy and Pandas: Libraries for Data Analysis

- **NumPy (Numerical Python):** NumPy is a fundamental library for scientific computing in Python. It provides efficient data structures like arrays and matrices, along with mathematical functions for numerical operations.

```python
import numpy as np

# Create a NumPy array
```

```python
data = np.array([1, 4, 2, 5])

# Perform calculations on the array
average = np.mean(data)
print(average)  # Output: 3.25
```

- **Pandas:** Pandas is a high-level library built on top of NumPy, specifically designed for data manipulation and analysis. It offers data structures like Series (one-dimensional) and DataFrames (two-dimensional labeled data) with powerful indexing, filtering, and transformation capabilities.

```python
import pandas as pd

# Create a pandas DataFrame from a dictionary
data = {"name": ["Alice", "Bob", "Charlie"], "age": [25, 30, 22]}
df = pd.DataFrame(data)

# Access data by column name
```

```
print(df["age"])  # Output: Series containing age data
```

By combining NumPy's numerical strength with Pandas' data manipulation capabilities, you can efficiently work with structured data for analysis.

8.2 Data Cleaning and Preprocessing Techniques

Real-world data often contains missing values, inconsistencies, and errors. Data cleaning and preprocessing are crucial steps to prepare your data for analysis and machine learning models. Common techniques include:

- **Handling Missing Values:**

    ○ **Imputation:** Filling missing values with statistical methods (mean, median) or carrying forward/backward values based on context.

    ○ **Deletion:** Removing rows/columns with too many missing values if appropriate.

- **Dealing with Outliers:** Identifying and handling extreme data points that might skew analysis. Techniques include winsorization (capping outliers to specific values) or removal if justified.

- **Encoding Categorical Data:** Converting categorical variables (text labels) into numerical representations suitable for machine learning algorithms. Common methods include one-hot encoding and label encoding.

```
# Example: Imputing missing values with mean
(assuming numerical data)
import numpy as np

data = np.array([1, 4, np.nan, 5])
mean_value = np.nanmean(data)  # Calculate the mean ignoring NaN
data[np.isnan(data)] = mean_value  # Impute missing values
```

```
print(data)  # Output: [ 1.  4.  2.5  5. ]
```

Data cleaning and preprocessing ensure the quality and consistency of your data, leading to more reliable analysis and model performance.

8.3 Exploratory Data Analysis (EDA): Exploring and Visualizing Data

Exploratory data analysis (EDA) involves summarizing, visualizing, and understanding your data to identify patterns, trends, and relationships. Common techniques include:

- **Descriptive Statistics:** Calculating measures like mean, median, standard deviation, and frequency distributions to get a basic understanding of the data.
- **Data Visualization:** Creating visualizations like histograms, scatter plots, box plots, and heatmaps to explore relationships between variables and identify potential outliers.

```python
import pandas as pd
import matplotlib.pyplot as plt

# Load sample data (replace with your data)
data = pd.read_csv("data.csv")

# Distribution of a numerical variable (age)
plt.hist(data["age"])
plt.xlabel("Age")
plt.ylabel("Number of People")
plt.title("Distribution of Age in the Data")
plt.show()

# Relationship between two variables (age and salary)
plt.scatter(data["age"], data["salary"])
plt.xlabel("Age")
plt.ylabel("Salary")
plt.title("Relationship Between Age and Salary")
plt.show()
```

Effective EDA helps you gain insights into your data, formulate hypotheses, and guide further analysis or machine learning tasks.

8.4 Introduction to Machine Learning: Basic Concepts and Algorithms

Machine learning (ML) allows computers to learn from data without explicit programming. Here are some fundamental concepts:

- **Supervised Learning:** In supervised learning, you provide the model with labeled data (inputs and desired outputs) and train it to learn a mapping between them. The model can then be used to predict outputs for new, unseen data. Examples include classification (predicting categories) and regression (predicting continuous values).

- **Unsupervised Learning:** In unsupervised learning, the data is unlabeled. The goal is to uncover hidden patterns or structures within the data itself. Common unsupervised learning tasks include clustering (grouping similar data points) and dimensionality reduction (compressing data while retaining important information).

- **Machine Learning Models:** Machine learning models are algorithms trained on data to perform specific tasks. Popular models include:

  - **Linear Regression:** Predicts a continuous output based on a linear relationship with input features.
  - **Logistic Regression:** Classifies data points into two categories (e.g., spam/not spam).
  - **Decision Trees:** Classifies data by making a series of yes/no decisions based on features.
  - **Support Vector Machines (SVMs):** Classifies data by finding a hyperplane that best separates data points of different classes.
  - **K-Means Clustering:** Groups data points into a predefined number of clusters based on their similarity.

- **Training, Validation, and Testing:** The data is typically split into training, validation, and testing sets. The model is trained on the training data, its performance is evaluated on the validation set to fine-tune hyperparameters (model parameters), and finally, the final performance is assessed on the unseen testing set.

8.5 Beyond the Basics: Additional Tools and Libraries

- **Scikit-learn:** A comprehensive library for machine learning algorithms, data preprocessing, and model evaluation.
- **Matplotlib, Seaborn:** Powerful libraries for creating various data visualizations.
- **TensorFlow, PyTorch:** Deep learning frameworks enabling the development and training of complex neural network models.

These libraries offer extensive functionalities for tackling various data science challenges.

Python provides a rich ecosystem of libraries and frameworks that make it a compelling choice for data science. By mastering these tools and concepts, you can unlock the power of data analysis and build intelligent applications that learn and adapt from data.

CHAPTER 9

AUTOMATION WITH PYTHON

Python excels at automating repetitive tasks, saving you time and effort. This chapter explores tools and techniques for automating various workflows.

9.1 Scripting: Automating Repetitive Tasks

- **Scripts:** Python scripts are programs written in a file (.py) that automate specific tasks. You can execute them from the command line or integrate them into other programs.

```
# Example script: rename all files in a directory (replace
logic as needed)
import os

directory = "data"
for filename in os.listdir(directory):
```

```
        new_filename    =    filename.replace(".txt",
"_processed.txt")
        os.rename(os.path.join(directory,    filename),
os.path.join(directory, new_filename))

    print("Files renamed successfully!")
```

- **Benefits of Scripting:**

  - **Saves Time:** Automate repetitive tasks instead of doing them manually.
  - **Reduces Errors:** Scripts minimize human error by following defined logic.
  - **Improves Consistency:** Scripts ensure tasks are performed consistently every time.
  - **Increases Efficiency:** Automate complex workflows for better efficiency.

By writing scripts, you can streamline your work and free yourself from tedious tasks.

9.2 Web Scraping with Beautiful Soup (or Scrapy): Extracting Data from Websites

- **Web Scraping:** Web scraping involves extracting data from websites. It can be useful for collecting information like product prices, news articles, or social media data (with ethical considerations and website permissions).

- **Beautiful Soup:**

  Beautiful Soup is a popular library for parsing HTML and XML content. It allows you to navigate the structure of a web page and extract specific data points.

```python
import requests
from bs4 import BeautifulSoup

url = "https://www.example.com/products"   # Replace with target URL
```

```python
# Download the webpage content
response = requests.get(url)
soup = BeautifulSoup(response.content, "html.parser")

# Find elements containing product information (adjust
selectors as needed)
products = soup.find_all("div", class_="product")

for product in products:
    # Extract product name and price (adjust based on
HTML structure)
    name = product.find("h2").text.strip()
    price = product.find("span", class_="price").text.strip()
    print(f"Product: {name}, Price: {price}")
```

- **Scrapy:** Scrapy is a robust framework for large-scale web scraping projects. It offers features like efficient crawling, data extraction rules, and handling dynamic websites.

Remember to respect website terms of service and robots.txt exclusions when scraping data.

9.3 Regular Expressions: Powerful Pattern Matching for Text Processing

- **Regular Expressions (Regex):** Regular expressions are powerful tools for pattern matching in text. They define patterns to search, extract, or replace specific text sequences.

```
import re

text = "My phone number is 123-456-7890 or 555-123-4567."

# Find all phone numbers using a regular expression
phone_pattern = r"\d{3}-\d{3}-\d{4}"   # Pattern for XXX-XXX-XXXX format
matches = re.findall(phone_pattern, text)
```

for match in matches:

print(f"Phone number found: {match}")

- **Applications of Regex:**

  - Extracting data from text (e.g., email addresses, URLs)
  - Validating user input formats (e.g., email address format)
  - Text cleaning and pre-processing tasks

Mastering regular expressions empowers you to manipulate text data efficiently.

9.4 Building Command-Line Tools: Creating Interactive Scripts

- **Command-Line Tools (CLIs):** CLIs allow users to interact with your script through the command line. You can add options, arguments, and error handling to create user-friendly tools.

```python
import argparse

def main():
    parser = argparse.ArgumentParser(description="File renamer script")
    parser.add_argument("--directory", required=True, help="Directory containing files to rename")
    parser.add_argument("--extension", default=".txt", help="File extension to rename (default: .txt)")
    parser.add_argument("--new_extension", default="_processed.txt", help="New file extension")
    args = parser.parse_args()

    # Implement file renaming logic using args.directory, args.extension, etc.

if __name__ == "__main__":
    main()
```

- **Benefits of CLIs (continued):**

- **Easy to Use:** Users can interact with your script without needing a graphical interface.

- **Automation Integration:** CLIs integrate well with other scripts and automation workflows.

- **Flexibility:** You can define various options and arguments for customization.

By creating CLIs, you make your scripts more versatile and accessible for users comfortable with the command line.

9.5 System Administration with Python

- **System Administration Tasks:** Python can automate various system administration tasks, including:

  - User and group management
  - File system management (creating, deleting, copying files/directories)
  - Process management (starting, stopping, monitoring processes)

○ Log file analysis and parsing

- **Libraries:** Libraries like os, shutil, subprocess, and psutil provide functionalities for interacting with the operating system.

Important: Use caution when automating system administration tasks, as unintended consequences can occur. It's recommended to test scripts thoroughly in controlled environments before deploying them in production.

9.6 Building Graphical User Interfaces (GUIs) with Python

- **Graphical User Interfaces (GUIs):** GUIs provide a visual interface for users to interact with your program. Python offers libraries like Tkinter (built-in) and PyQt for creating GUIs.

```python
# Example using Tkinter (basic example)
from tkinter import Tk, Label, Button

def greet():
  print("Hello, world!")

window = Tk()
window.title("My GUI Application")

label = Label(window, text="Welcome!")
label.pack()

button = Button(window, text="Click Me", command=greet)
button.pack()

window.mainloop()
```

While Tkinter provides a basic GUI toolkit, PyQt and other libraries offer more advanced features and customization options for building complex GUIs.

Python's versatility empowers you to automate various tasks, from simple scripting to web scraping, text processing, and even system administration. By leveraging the tools and libraries covered in this chapter, you can streamline your workflow, extract valuable data from websites, and build user-friendly applications for different purposes. Remember to prioritize responsible web scraping practices and exercise caution when automating system administration tasks.

CHAPTER 10

ADVANCED TOPICS

As you progress in your Python development journey, these advanced topics become essential for building robust, maintainable, and well-organized codebases.

10.1 Unit Testing: Writing Tests for Your Code

- **Unit Testing:** Unit testing involves writing small, focused programs that test individual units of your code (functions, classes, modules). It helps ensure that your code functions as expected and catches errors early in the development process.

- **Benefits of Unit Testing:**

  o **Improved Code Quality:** Tests identify bugs and regressions as you write code, leading to more reliable software.

- **Better Code Maintainability:** Well-written tests can document code behavior and clarify functionality.
- **Increased Confidence:** Tests provide assurance that your code works as intended, boosting development confidence.

-

- **Popular Unit Testing Frameworks in Python:**

  - **unittest:** The built-in Python unit testing framework.
  - **pytest:** A popular third-party framework known for its simplicity and flexibility.

```python
# Example using unittest (replace with your code)
import unittest

def add(x, y):
    """Returns the sum of two numbers."""
    return x + y
```

```python
class TestAdd(unittest.TestCase):
  def test_positive(self):
    result = add(2, 3)
    self.assertEqual(result, 5)

  def test_negative(self):
    result = add(-1, 4)
    self.assertEqual(result, 3)


if __name__ == "__main__":
  unittest.main()
```

By incorporating unit testing into your development workflow, you can write more reliable and maintainable Python code.

10.2 Debugging Techniques: Identifying and Fixing Errors

- **Debugging:** Debugging is the process of identifying and fixing errors in your code. It involves using various techniques to pinpoint the source of the error and implement a solution.

- **Common Debugging Techniques:**

  - **Print Statements:** Strategically placing print statements in your code helps inspect variable values and trace program execution.
  - **Debuggers:** Python includes a built-in debugger (pdb) that allows you to step through your code line by line, examining variables and expressions.
  - **Error Messages:** Pay close attention to error messages generated by Python. They often provide valuable clues about the location and nature of the error.

- **Debugging Tips:**

  - **Simplify:** Break down complex code into

smaller, testable units during debugging.

○ **Reproduce:** Try to replicate the error consistently to narrow down the issue.

○ **Search Online:** Leverage online resources and communities for solutions to common errors.

Effective debugging skills are crucial for resolving errors and enhancing your problem-solving abilities as a Python developer.

10.3 Version Control with Git: Managing Your Code Effectively

- **Version Control:** Version control systems like Git allow you to track changes to your code over time. You can revert to previous versions, collaborate with others, and manage different code branches for development and deployment.

- **Benefits of Version Control:**

- ○ **Track Changes:** See how your code has evolved over time and revert to previous versions if necessary.

- ○ **Collaboration:** Multiple developers can work on the same codebase simultaneously.

- ○ **Branching and Merging:** Create isolated branches for development, feature testing, and seamlessly merge changes back into the main codebase.

- • **Popular Version Control Systems (VCS):**

- ○ **Git:** A widely used distributed VCS offering powerful features and flexibility.

Learning Git and using a VCS is essential for managing code effectively, especially in collaborative development environments.

10.4 Deployment Strategies: Sharing Your Python Applications

- **Deployment:** Deployment refers to the process of making your Python application available to users in a production environment (e.g., web server, cloud platform).

- **Deployment Strategies:**

  ○ **Simple Scripting:** For smaller applications, you can deploy by copying your Python script and any dependencies to the target environment.

  ○ **Packaging Tools:** Tools like pyinstaller or cx_Freeze can create standalone executables of your application, making it easier to distribute.

  ○ **Web Frameworks:** Frameworks like Flask and Django often have deployment guides and tools specific to web applications.

○ **Cloud Platforms:** Cloud platforms like Heroku or AWS offer managed environments for deploying and scaling Python applications.

The deployment strategy you choose depends on the complexity of your application, infrastructure, and desired scalability.

Security considerations become more critical when deploying applications to production environments. Take appropriate measures to secure your code and user data.

By mastering the concepts covered in this chapter, you'll elevate your Python development skills. Unit testing ensures code quality, debugging techniques empower you to fix errors efficiently, version control with Git fosters collaboration and code management, and deployment strategies enable you to share your Python applications with the world. Remember, these practices contribute to building professional, well-maintained, and reliable Python software.

Here's a quick recap of the key takeaways from this chapter:

- **Unit Testing:** Write tests to verify individual units of your code, improving code quality and maintainability.

- **Debugging Techniques:** Utilize print statements, debuggers, and error messages to identify and fix errors effectively.

- **Version Control with Git:** Track code changes, collaborate with others, and manage branches using Git or a VCS for efficient code management.

- **Deployment Strategies:** Choose a deployment strategy (scripting, packaging tools, web frameworks, cloud platforms) that aligns with your application's needs and infrastructure.

- **Security Considerations:** Prioritize security measures to protect code and user data during production deployment.

This chapter concludes our exploration of Python's vast capabilities. As you continue your Python journey, remember to practice, experiment, and explore new libraries and frameworks. The Python community is vast and welcoming, so don't hesitate to seek help and learn from others. With dedication and continuous learning, you can leverage Python's power to create innovative and impactful applications.

ABOUT THE AUTHOR

Writer's Bio:

 Benjamin Evans, a respected figure in the tech world, is known for his insightful commentary and analysis. With a strong educational background likely in fields such as computer science, engineering, or business, he brings a depth of knowledge to his discussions on emerging technologies and industry trends. Evans' knack for simplifying complex concepts, coupled with his innate curiosity and passion for innovation, has established him as a go-to source for understanding the dynamics of the digital landscape. Through articles, speeches, and social media, he shares his expertise and offers valuable insights into the impact of technology on society.

www.ingramcontent.com/pod-product-compliance
Lightning Source LLC
LaVergne TN
LVHW051710050326
832903LV00032B/4126

ISBN 9798325330230

90000

9 798325 330230